❧ HISPANIC AMERICA ❧

THE
NEW REPUBLIC
1760~1840s

BY

STEVEN OTFINOSKI

Marshall Cavendish
Benchmark
New York

Thanks to Stephen Pitti, professor of history and American studies at Yale University, for his expert reading of this manuscript.

MARSHALL CAVENDISH BENCHMARK
99 WHITE PLAINS ROAD
TARRYTOWN, NEW YORK 10591-5502
www.marshallcavendish.us

LIBRARY OF CONGRESS CATALOGING-IN-PUBLICATION DATA
Otfinoski, Steven.
The New Republic / by Steven Otfinoski.
p. cm. — (Hispanic America)
Includes bibliographical references and index.
Summary: "Provides comprehensive information on the history of the Spanish exploring the United States"—Provided by publisher.
ISBN 978-0-7614-2938-8
1. Hispanic Americans—History—18th century—Juvenile literature.
2. Hispanic Americans—History—19th century—Juvenile literature.
3. Spaniards—United States—History—18th century—Juvenile literature.
4. Spaniards—United States—History—19th century—Juvenile literature.
5. United States—History—Revolution, 1775-1783—Participation, Spanish—Juvenile literature.
6. Florida—History—Spanish colony, 1784-1821—Juvenile literature.
7. Mexico—History—Wars of Independence, 1810-1821—Juvenile literature.
8. Mexican-American Border Region—History—19th century. I. Title.
E184.S75O84 2009
973.30896'1—dc22
2007045958

Photo research by Linda Sykes

Cover photo: Benjamin Franklin a the Constitutional Convention of 1787. He was instrumental in bringing together warring factions within the new republic. Back Cover photo: The Granger Collection

The photographs in this book are used by permission and through the courtesy of:
The Art Archive: Natural History Museum, Mexico City/Dagli Orti, 1; Bibliotheque des Arts Decoratifs, Paris/Dagli Orti, 13; Natural History Museum, Mexico City/Dagli Orti, 18, 20-21. *The Granger Collection:* 4, 8, 10, 14-15, 27, 35, 38, 40, 43, 45, 46, 48, 51, 53, 54, 59, 68, 70. Louisiana State Museum, 24. *Corbis:* 30, 69, 71. *The Bridgeman Art Library:* Museo de America, Madrid, Spain, 32; Bolivar Museum, Caracas, Venezuela/Giraudon, 42. California Military Museum, 56. Witte Museum, 58. *Bettmann/Corbis,* 60. *Alamy:* Lebrecht Archive of Music and Art, 62. Museum of New Mexico, 64. *Art Resource, NY:* Smithsonian American Art Museum, Washington, D. C., 67.

EDITOR: Joy Bean   PUBLISHER: Michelle Bisson
ART DIRECTOR: Anahid Hamparian   SERIES DESIGNER: Kristen Branch

Printed in China
1 3 5 6 4 2

Contents

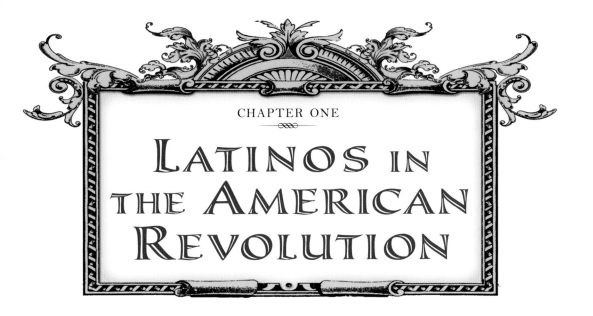

CHAPTER ONE

LATINOS IN THE AMERICAN REVOLUTION

SPAIN HAD BEEN EXPLORING AND COLONIZING the Americas since Christopher Columbus's historic first voyage to the New World in 1492. It was soon joined by the major European powers of France and Great Britain, who established their own colonies in the New World. France and Great Britain fought each other in a series of wars in both North America and Europe for dominance in the New World. The last of these wars, the Seven Years' War (1756–1763), ended in British victory (in America, the war was known as the French and Indian War). France's defeat ended its role as a major colonial power in America.

The period from 1760 to 1830 was one of enormous change in both the British and Spanish colonies in North and

Opposite: In the 1740s, Great Britain fought to establish colonies, like this one in Cape Breton Island in Nova Scotia, which Britain gained after the French surrendered it.

South America. With the support of France and Spain, the American colonists rebelled against Great Britain and won their independence. During this same period, the Spanish borderlands of New Mexico, Texas, and California grew and developed, although at a slower pace than Mexico to the south. And Florida, a former Spanish colony in British hands for twenty years, was returned to Spain at the end of the American Revolution.

The struggle for freedom that led to the formation of the United States reverberated in the Spanish colonies, especially Mexico, and it soon began its own fight for independence from Spain. During this ongoing struggle, the people in the borderlands of Spanish America were searching for their own identity. The newly formed nation of the United States, as well as the nation of Mexico to the south, were New Republics. The republic of Mexico welcomed American settlers in New Mexico and Texas, until their growing numbers became a threat. As the period of nation-building drew to a close in the early 1830s, the common bonds that had joined the Latino countries and the former British colonies were being pulled apart by the growing nationalism of the Mexican and American republics.

THE CALL OF FREEDOM

Under the Peace Treaty of Paris, which ended the Seven Years' War, France lost Canada and all its territory east of the Mississippi River to Great Britain. Spain, France's ally in the war, lost Florida to Britain. To compensate Spain for its losses and to keep its colony of Louisiana out of British hands, France secretly gave Louisiana to Spain. This included all French territory west of the Mississippi as well as the city of New Orleans at the mouth of the Mississippi on the Gulf of Mexico. Also under the treaty, the British agreed to return Havana, capital of the Spanish island colony of Cuba, to Spain.

The American colonies experienced a similar sense of loss and gain after the war. Although they were grateful to Great Britain for ending the threat of the French and their Native-American allies, the colonists were unhappy with the new taxes the British levied against them to help pay the enormous cost of the war. As resistance to these taxes grew, the British clamped down on colonial freedom. This only worsened the situation. By 1775, a third of the colonial population was prepared to rebel against the motherland. They formed their own Continental Congress in Philadelphia, Pennsylvania. The following year, after the first shedding of blood at Lexington and Concord in Massachusetts, the congress issued the Declaration of Independence. It stated the colonies' grievances against the British king and formally declared their independence from British rule. It was, in a sense, a declaration of war. The American Revolution had begun.

Early Spanish Aid to the Colonies

No sooner had war been declared than the Spanish began to supply aid to the rebellious American patriots. Why did they do so? A great part of the answer lies more with Spain's intense dislike for Great Britian than with its friendship with the colonists. Although France, who also supported the colonial cause, was no longer a power in North America, Spain remained a major colonial player and Britain's main competitor. It claimed all of South America, except for Portuguese Brazil; many of the islands in the Caribbean; Mexico (known

The Declaration Committee of 1776 was composed of (l. to r.) Benjamin Franklin, Thomas Jefferson, Robert R. Livingston, John Adams, and Roger Sherman.

as New Spain); and most of what is now the southwestern United States, including California. Spain longed to drive the British out of the eastern seaboard as well as the Caribbean, where they preyed on Spanish colonies. Spain also was eager to win back Florida from the British.

No sooner had the ink dried on the Declaration of Independence than Virginian George Gibson set off from Fort Pitt (now Pittsburgh) down the Mississippi River to New Orleans. On his arrival, he gave a secret communiqué to Louisiana governor Don Luis de Unzaga asking for gun supplies, and gunpowder. Unzaga was a fair and progressive governor and he sympathized with the American patriots. Because Spain was officially neutral in the Revolution, Unzaga had Gibson publicly arrested as a trespasser, but secretly he shipped 9,000 pounds (4,082 kilograms) of gunpowder upriver to Fort Pitt and another 1,000 pounds (453.6 kg) by ship to Philadelphia.

Encouraged by this display of Spanish support, the Continental Congress sent a three-man delegation led by Benjamin Franklin to Spain to formally request Spanish aid. King Carlos III responded favorably to the request and gave one million British pounds to the rebels, which was used to buy everything from cannons to soldiers' uniforms.

In 1777, Spanish delegate and merchant Juan de Miralles sailed from Cuba to Philadelphia to establish official diplomatic relations between Spain and the Continental Congress. Miralles was an able diplomat who spoke English, French, and Spanish. He quickly gained the trust and respect of American leaders, especially General George Washington, commander of the Continental Army. When Miralles became ill and died in 1780 while visiting Washington at Morristown, New Jersey, the American general attended his funeral.

A NEW GOVERNOR IN LOUISIANA

Bernardo de Gálvez arrived in Louisiana in 1777, and soon after replaced Unzaga as governor. Gálvez was the nephew of

José de Gálvez, head administrator of all Spanish colonies in the Americas. This was Bernardo's second tour of the Americas. In 1762, while still in his teens, he had fought the Apache Indians in Mexico and was wounded more than once. Returning to Spain, he was sent to serve in France and in Algeria in northern Africa.

As governor, Gálvez was remarkably different from the men who preceded him, including Unzaga. He did not look down on the *Creoles* of New Orleans and got along well with them. He even married a young Creole widow, Marie Felice de Saint-Maxent Estrehan, with whom he had three children. Although previous administrators had feared the neighboring British in Florida, who outnumbered the people of Louisiana, Gálvez was not intimidated. He admired the American patriots for going to war against the British and saw their struggle as a means for Spain to reclaim Florida.

Bernardo de Gálvez was known as a fair and kind ruler.

In defiance of the British, Gálvez secretly opened the port of New Orleans to the Americans. He pretended to detain their ships while the British watched but, once they had left, he released them. He gave aid to the Americans with money and supplies. The British learned of these activities through their spies, however, and Gálvez received word that British soldiers stationed in forts along the lower Mississippi and the Gulf of Mexico were planning to launch an attack on Louisiana. Then, on June 21, 1779, Spain declared war on Britain and officially recognized the *sovereignty* of the American colonies.

At War in the Gulf

Gálvez did not wait for the British to attack him. He attacked them first, hoping to weaken British control in Florida. He assembled a small army of Spaniards and Creoles and on August 27, 1779, marched 90 miles (144.8 km) north toward the British fort at Manchac. Along the way, Gálvez stopped at every settlement and signed up new recruits. They included French, Creoles, Anglos, freed African slaves, and even Native Americans who opposed the British. By the time he reached Manchac in early September, Gálvez had doubled the size of his army. The fort, much to his surprise, was a rotting edifice, defended by only two dozen soldiers. Most of them fled at the first gunfire, and the Spanish took the fort with little resistance.

Emboldened by this first success, Gálvez moved on to the British fort at Baton Rouge. This fort was defended by many more British soldiers, however, and had thick walls and a surrounding ditch to hold off attackers. But Gálvez was not discouraged. Instead of launching a straightforward attack on the fort, he planned a diversion. He sent a small band made up mostly of Native Americans to build a barricade near a grove of trees on one side of the fort. While the British bombarded the grove, the main part of the army was setting up defenses on the opposite side of the fort. The next morning, the British realized too late that they had been fooled. The battle lasted only a few hours before the fort surrendered. As part of the negotiations, Gálvez demanded the surrender of the British fort at Natchez, which took place soon after.

It was a stunning string of victories. Gálvez had captured more than a thousand British soldiers in three forts, and he had broken the British hold on the lower Mississippi River Valley. The American patriots could now receive needed supplies from New Orleans via the Mississippi River and continue their fight. It was a major turning point in the American Revolution. Gálvez had done all this, and his army had suffered only one fatality and two wounded.

THE BATTLE OF PENSACOLA

Gálvez next looked to conquer the Florida coast along the Gulf of Mexico, which was still a British stronghold. Florida had been divided into two colonies by the British. East Florida was the main peninsula of the present-day state. West Florida consisted of part of the Florida panhandle and continued west across the Gulf coasts of present-day Alabama, Mississippi, and Louisiana. West Florida was defended by two formidable British forts at Mobile and Pensacola, the colony's capital. In January 1780, Gálvez sailed in a small fleet carrying an army of 754 men along the coast to Mobile Bay. Some 567 more Spanish troops sailing from Havana, Cuba, joined his force at Mobile on February 10. The fort and city fell in five days. Upon hearing of Gálvez's victory, King Carlos promoted Gálvez to field marshal, presiding over all military operations against the British in North America.

Gálvez and his troops sailed from Havana (seen here) to attack the British at Pensacola Bay.

But the biggest prize, Pensacola, was still under British control. Two forts on Pensacola Bay defended the capital. Knowing he would need a larger force to take the city, Gálvez sailed to Havana to persuade the reluctant Cuban governor to give him more men. When he finally returned to New Orleans, after weather delays, he had an army totaling seven thousand soldiers. They made up one of the most diverse international fighting forces in the New World and included Cubans, Mexicans, Haitians, Native Americans, Santo Dominicans, and Venezuelans.

Gálvez entered Pensacola Bay with a small force. A larger accompanying Spanish fleet, fearing the British guns, hung back. A frustrated Gálvez sent the fleet's admiral a note that read: "Whoever has valor and honor will follow me." The admiral was shamed into action and followed. The British fired on the invaders. A siege began that lasted sixty-five days. Finally, a well-aimed Spanish shell struck the British powder storage and it exploded into flames. Two

Bernardo de Gálvez captured Pensacola from the British in 1781.

LATINOS IN THE AMERICAN REVOLUTION

days later, the British surrendered. It was Gálvez's greatest victory and one of the most important battles of the entire Revolutionary War. The Spanish took one thousand British prisoners. In both of the battles he fought in West Florida, Gálvez lost a total of just 124 men with another 247 wounded. The king made Gálvez, the victor of Pensacola, a count. He called for Gálvez's coat of arms to bear the likeness of a single ship with the inscription *Yo Solo*, meaning I alone.

FINAL VICTORY

In 1782, Gálvez led a fleet that captured another British naval base at New Providence in the Bahamian Islands. He was preparing to attack the one remaining British base in the Gulf of Mexico on the island of Jamaica when word reached him that the British and the Americans were working on a peace settlement. The final American victory was in no small part due to the efforts of Bernardo de Gálvez and the bold men who fought with him.

Gálvez was an active participant in the Peace Treaty of Paris in 1783. Under the treaty, the American colonies gained their independence, and the British gave to Spain both East and West Florida. Gálvez was a great hero both in Spain and in the new republic of the United States. Two *parishes*, or counties in Louisiana, were named after him and his wife. A group of Anglo Americans settled a town along the Gulf coast of Texas and named it Galveztown in his honor. Today it is known as the city of Galveston.

Gálvez was appointed governor of Cuba in 1784. His father, the *viceroy* of New Spain, died soon after, and his son was named his successor. Gálvez arrived in Mexico City, the capital, in June 1785. He became as popular there as he had been in Louisiana. When famine and plague struck in 1786, Gálvez donated a portion of his inheritance to buy food for starving residents. He improved life in Mexico City by installing streetlights and building a highway to Acapulco on the Pacific coast. His popularity with the people made the Spanish authorities resentful and jealous. They did not trust Gálvez and even feared that the democratic spirit he encouraged would lead to rebellions in their colonies. The Crown issued a rebuke of the governor. A disillusioned Gálvez then came down with the dreaded disease of malaria and died on November 30, 1786.

Most of the men who succeeded Gálvez in colonial government did not follow his example. Instead, they kept firm control on the people and stifled any spirit of independence. The revolution that the authorities feared would rob them of their colonies eventually came. In time, the citizens of the new republic, which Spain had helped achieve its independence, would become an even greater threat to its colonial empire than the British had been.

THE SECOND RISE AND FALL OF SPANISH FLORIDA

IN 1783, WITH THEIR REVOLUTION WON, THE Continental Congress passed a resolution bestowing on King Carlos III of Spain the title Powerful Protector and Defender of the Independence of the United States. But it would not be long before Spain, the new republic's friend, would need the United States' protection.

Spanish Florida remained the only part of the eastern seaboard of the new United States that did not belong to the new republic. As it established itself and elected George Washington its first president in 1789, Americans began to move beyond the original thirteen colonies. Many headed west, while others in the southeast moved into sparsely populated West Florida.

Opposite:
King Carlos III of Spain supported the United States as it fought against the British in the Revolutionary War.

There were several reasons why Florida was not widely settled. When the British left in 1783, many British traders and American *Tories* of the Revolution left with them. Even Saint Augustine, the oldest white settlement in North America, shrank from a population of 17,000 to about 3,000 almost overnight. Most of the Spanish settlers had left twenty years earlier when the British took over, and few were interested in returning. Much of West and East Florida was a no-man's-land, its swamps and lowlands a refuge for runaway African slaves and prisoners as well as pirates. Native Americans, especially Seminoles, used Florida as a base from which to conduct raids on Americans living in Georgia, the southernmost American state at that time.

A MELTING POT

In 1784, a new governor, Vincente Manuel de Zéspedes, was named in East Florida. Like Gálvez, Zéspedes was that rarity among the rigid officials

In New York,
George
Washington
was inaugurated
as the first
president of the
United States
in 1789.

of colonial Spain, a progressive. He knew that the colony could not survive without committed settlers. He invited immigrants from Spain, as well as from other European countries, to colonize in East Florida. He even welcomed Anglo-American settlers if they were willing to become Spanish citizens. Along with these groups were British traders who had stayed and runaway slaves looking for a new life. This influx of different peoples turned Florida into as great a melting pot as New Orleans was.

But the Spanish authorities were determined to keep the influx under control. They refused to allow Florida colonists to trade with anyone but Spain. Zéspedes laxly enforced these trade laws, but his subjects still resented their existence. Colonists in Florida wanted to be free to sell and trade with whomever they wished. Anglo-American settlers pressured the United States to *annex* West Florida, the more vulnerable of the two colonies. A border dispute began in 1784, however, when the United States government argued that the border of Florida was the 31st parallel. The Spanish insisted it lay 100 miles (160 km) north of the parallel.

Spain's attention, however, was becoming more and more focused on events in Europe. The French Revolution (1789–1799), which overthrew King Louis XVI, was seen as a serious threat to all the monarchies of Europe, including Spain. Spain joined its neighbors in a series of wars against the French revolutionaries, which spread across the European continent. The Spanish had little time or energy to devote to their colonies 3,000 miles (4,828 km) away, including those in Florida. In 1795, Spain surrendered to American demands and signed a treaty making the 31st parallel Florida's northern border. It also allowed the United States free use of the lower Mississippi River for trade and commerce.

LAST DAYS OF SPANISH LOUISIANA

West of Spanish Florida, Louisiana was also experiencing problems with the Anglos to the north. King Louis XV of France had secretly given Louisiana to his cousin King Carlos III of Spain in 1762 to prevent it from falling into British hands. Unlike the British in Florida, the French residents of New Orleans and the surrounding area were not about to leave their homes when the Spanish took over. They were so opposed to Spanish rule, though, that they drove out the Spanish commissioner, Antonio de Ulloa, two years after his arrival in 1768 and declared Louisiana an independent country. Spain retaliated by sending over a formidable force that quelled the rebellion and captured and executed its ringleaders.

Spanish Commissioner Antonio de Ulloa was driven out of Louisiana before it was declared an independent country.

SPANISH NEW ORLEANS

New Orleans was already the most distinctive city in North America when the Spanish took it over in 1766. It was founded as a fort by French explorer Jean Baptiste Le Moyne Beinville (pictured above) in 1718 and soon was named the capital of the French territory of Louisiana. Located just

100 miles (160 km) north of the mouth of the Mississippi River, New Orleans became a major port for goods coming from the north on flat-boats and barges and from ships carrying foreign goods through the Gulf of Mexico.

The Creole population of New Orleans was surprisingly mixed for the time. It included whites of French and Spanish heritage, those of mixed French-Spanish heritage, *mulattos* of mixed European and African descent, and African Americans. They all got along well and there was little discrimination. Spain brought its laws and currency to New Orleans, but in most other respects it remained stubbornly Creole French. French aristocrats fleeing the French Revolution also settled in the city, reflecting an old-world elegance in elaborate masked balls and lavish entertainments. But there was another, darker side to New Orleans. Unsanitary conditions, a humid climate, and foreign sailors brought disease to the city. Periodic epidemics of plague, yellow fever, and cholera took thousands of lives. Fires were another constant danger. The great fire of March 21, 1788, burned almost the entire city to the ground. The hearty people of New Orleans rebuilt it, replacing wooden houses and buildings with stone ones. France took Louisiana back from Spain in 1880.

When the French sold the city and all Louisiana to the United States in 1803, the population doubled to around eight thousand people in just seven years. But even under the enterprising Americans, New Orleans remained an international city, true to its French and Spanish roots.

A later Louisiana governor, Esteban Miró, was a more enlightened administrator, like Zéspedes in Florida. He resisted enforcing new regulations that closed the lower Mississippi River and the port of New Orleans to American traders. In 1788, he persuaded the Spanish Crown to offer Anglo Americans free land grants in the fertile Mississippi River Valley if they agreed to become Spanish citizens. This program was successful, and Louisiana's population doubled between 1782 and 1792.

But the days of Spanish Louisiana were numbered. Out of the turmoil of the French Revolution emerged a new military leader, Napoleon Bonaparte. Napoleon made himself emperor of France and looked to repossess the vast territory of Louisiana that France had years earlier given away to Spain. Napoleon forced King Carlos IV to give Louisiana back to France in 1800. He planned to make Louisiana the hub of a new French empire in the Americas, stretching from upper Louisiana to the Caribbean. But a bloody rebellion on the French island colony of San Domingo, now Haiti, which had broken out in 1791, disrupted Napoleon's plans. Napoleon sent a French army to put down the revolution in 1799. By 1802, however, more than 24,000 French soldiers had died on San Domingo, many of them from yellow fever. The French were unable to end the Haitian slave rebellion while embroiled in a war with Britain over control of Egypt and other colonial holdings. The war ended briefly in 1802 but started up again the following year. Napoleon

A Haitian revolt broke out in San Domingo in 1791, as depicted here.

was running low on money to wage his European wars and decided to give up his dream of an American empire. He knew the Americans were interested in buying part of Louisiana. The president of the United States, Thomas Jefferson, had authorized his agent, Robert Livingston, to offer the French up to 10 million dollars for New Orleans and the small section of Louisiana next to West Florida. In April 1803, Livingston got the shock of his life when

Napoleon offered him all of Louisiana, a 828,000-square-mile (2,144,520-sq-km) region stretching from New Orleans to the Rocky Mountains. The offer was accepted, and the United States paid 15 million dollars for an area that doubled the size of the nation. At three cents an acre, the Louisiana Purchase was one of the best real estate deals in American history.

THE ANNEXATION OF WEST FLORIDA

President Jefferson offered to buy West Florida from Spain as part of the Louisiana Purchase, but Spain refused. Over the next seven years, American settlers continued to pour into West Florida. In 1810, a band of Americans captured the Spanish fort at Baton Rouge and declared the region the Republic of West Florida. That October, U.S. president James Madison officially annexed a chunk of West Florida from the Mississippi River to the Perdido River. Spain, still reeling from the Napoleonic wars, was too weak to do more than verbally protest the United States' actions.

In 1812, a second war broke out between the British and the Americans, called the War of 1812. Spain allowed its former foe, Britain, to use Pensacola as a naval base during that war. This angered the Americans, and in 1814, U.S. general Andrew Jackson led a militia into Florida and seized Pensacola. The War of 1812 ended with the British being driven out of America, but the Spanish continued to cling stubbornly, if tentatively, to East Florida.

General Jackson Invades Florida Again

The United States was looking for an excuse to take the rest of Florida from the Spanish, and they found it in 1817. Seminole Indians were crossing the U.S. border to raid settlements, burn homes, and kill American citizens. The situation was complicated by the fact that the Seminoles had been instigated by two British fur traders and adventurers, Alexander Arbuthnot and Robert Ambrister. The U.S. government ordered General Jackson, one of the heroes of the War of 1812, to hunt down the marauding Seminoles, even if it meant crossing into Spanish Florida to do it.

In 1818, Jackson led a force of Tennessee militiamen into Florida, burning and pillaging every Native-American village in their path. He then proceeded, without authorization, to capture the Spanish forts of Saint Marks and Pensacola. He caught the British traders Arbuthnot and Ambrister, along with two Seminole leaders. Jackson court-martialed and executed the two British citizens. He also executed the two Seminoles without a trial. Then, with the Spanish governor having fled Pensacola, Jackson boldly pulled down the Spanish flag and replaced it with the American flag. The British quickly conceded that Arbuthnot and Ambrister got what they deserved, but the Spanish protested Jackson's actions. U.S. president James Monroe and Secretary of State John Quincy Adams defended Jackson, arguing that the Spanish failed to control

A painting
depicting
Andrew Jackson
and his troops
during his
invasion of
Pensacola in
1818.

the activities of those living in their colony, leaving Jackson
no recourse but to take action himself.

THE ADAMS–ONÍS TREATY

The Spanish realized that they were on the verge of losing
Florida and rather than have the Americans simply take it
from them, they decided to sell it. On February 22, 1819,
Secretary Adams and Spanish minister Luis de Onís
signed a treaty. The Adams-Onís Treaty called for Spain to
surrender all of Florida along with its claim to the Oregon
region on the Pacific coast, north of Spanish California. In
return, the United States would pay up to 5 million dollars

to all Americans whose property had been destroyed by Seminole raids from Spanish Florida. The United States would also renounce all claims to another Spanish province where Americans were settling in large numbers—Texas.

The actual surrendering of Florida took place in 1821. That same year, Spain would lose a far greater prize, not to the United States, but to their own colonists. Mexico, after years of struggle, was about to declare its independence.

CHAPTER THREE

THE LONG ROAD TO MEXICAN INDEPENDENCE

B Y 1790, MEXICO HAD BEEN UNDER SPANISH rule for three centuries, about twice as long as the American colonies had been ruled by Great Britain before they gained independence. Although there had been humane government leaders and missionary priests who tried to meet the needs of the people they ruled, the official Spanish policy allowed for little freedom or representation within the strictly structured society. *Peninsulares*, people born in Spain but residing in Mexico, held all the important government positions and owned the largest estates. *Criollos*, Mexicans born of Spanish parents, could not hold public office, but could own businesses and farms. The vast majority

Opposite:
A mixed-race marriage: a male Spaniard and his Mexican-Indian wife, and their child, a mestiza.

of Mexicans were *mestizos*, people of mixed Native American and Spanish blood, and *indios,* full-blooded Native Americans. They were mostly poor, uneducated, and often worked for wealthy *peninsulares* or criollos. Resentment among the mass of Mexicans toward the ruling class ran deep. The flames of rebellion were fed by the successes of the American Revolution, the French Revolution, and the slave rebellion in Santo Domingo, which had resulted in the republic of Haiti declaring its independence in 1804.

THE CRY OF DOLORES

A small band of Mexican revolutionaries were led by Father Miguel Hidalgo y Costilla, a sixty-year-old priest who lived in the small town of Dolores. Although a criollo, Father Hidalgo identified with the poor and downtrodden. Early on the morning of September 16, 1810, he rang the town's church bells. When a crowd of people had gathered, he delivered a fiery speech, condemning the Spaniards and calling for Mexican independence. He ended his speech with the cry "Long live Mexico!" This *Grito de Dolores* (Cry of Dolores) was as stirring a rallying cry for rebellion as the shot heard 'round the world at Lexington and Concord, where the first skirmishes of the American Revolution took place. With two other revolutionary leaders, Hidalgo gathered an army of mestizos and indios. Armed only with axes, pitchforks, and clubs, the rebel army marched the 120 miles (193 km) south to Mexico

Father Miguel
Hidalgo y
Costilla shouts
his famous Cry
of Dolores,
which stirred
rebellion.

THE LONG ROAD TO MEXICAN INDEPENDENCE

City, gathering more recruits at every village along the way. By the time they approached the capital, Hidalgo's army was 80,000 strong.

On a hill just outside the city, the army clashed with Spanish troops and defeated them. With his men exhausted from fighting, Hidalgo led them to the city of Guadalajara to rest and regroup. This gave the Spaniards a chance to pull together an army of professionally trained soldiers with superior weapons. In a second battle, the Spanish army crushed the rebel forces. Father Hidalgo fled and was later captured. On July 30, 1811, he was executed by a firing squad. Before he died, he blessed the men who were about to kill him and vowed that Mexico would one day be free. Today, Father Hidalgo is revered as the Father of Mexican Independence. September 16, the day he declared his revolt, is still celebrated as Mexico's Independence Day.

The revolutionary leadership then passed to another priest and Hidalgo supporter, Father José Maria Morelos y Parón. He trained his volunteer soldiers well, equipping them with guns taken from the Spaniards. Morelos's army captured the key port city of Acapulco. However, Morelos soon realized that he could not win against large numbers of professional Spanish soldiers and changed his tactics. He trained his followers in guerilla warfare, attacking without warning with small effective bands of fighters in enemy territory, capturing small towns and villages.

The liberal reforms that Morelos promoted struck terror in the hearts of most criollos and peninsulares. They did not want all Mexicans to be equal and allowed to own property, regardless of race and social standing. They felt that Morelos's government would take away the power and authority both of the army and the Roman Catholic Church, institutions these privileged groups saw as necessary to keep the social order. The criollos and peninsulares turned their backs on Morelos and gave their support to the Spanish Crown. Morelos was captured in November 1815 and executed a month later. For the next five years, the revolution was only kept alive by small bands of guerilla fighters who hid in the mountains.

THE REVOLUTION IS WON

In 1820, Spain experienced its own small rebellion when liberals in the government briefly removed King Ferdinand VII from office. Royalists in Mexico that were loyal to the king ordered Spanish military leader Agustín de Iturbide to crush the Mexican rebellion, now led by Vicente Guerrero. Iturbide and some members of the Mexican ruling class felt that the revolution could not be stopped, but they believed that it could be controlled. If they took the reins of the rebellion, the group reasoned, they could steer it away from the liberal republic that the revolutionaries wanted and still keep their privileges and power in an independent Mexico.

LEONA VICARIO

Not all members of the ruling class opposed the Mexican struggle for independence. Leona Vicario was born into a wealthy family in 1789, but as a young woman she became committed to Father Hidalgo and his cause. From her home in Mexico City, Vicario provided the rebels with money for supplies and intelligence. She was finally exposed, arrested, and imprisoned by the Spanish, but she managed to escape. She fled to the rebels' camp and served for several years as a nurse for the wounded. She met and fell in love with revolutionary leader Andres Quintana Roos, and the couple married. Both of them were pardoned by the Spanish government in 1819, but they continued to support independence, which was achieved two years later. The legislators of Coahula province in northern Mexico honored Vicario in 1827, changing the name of their capital from Saltillo to Leona Vicario. She died in 1842 and is buried with her husband in the Independence Column, a famous landmark in Mexico City.

A scene depicting Agustín de Iturbide entering Mexico City in September 1821.

So Iturbide, whose orders were to fight Guerrero, ended up joining forces with him. After years of violence and death, the final act of independence was surprisingly bloodless. The majority of Mexicans and Spaniards in the country supported the movement, and independence was declared on February 24, 1821. The only fighting that followed that year took place between Mexican troops and a few Spanish forces that remained loyal to Spain. In July, Spanish viceroy Juan O'Donoju landed at Veracruz and was denied entry into Mexico City until he agreed to sign the Treaty of Córdoba, officially recognizing Mexico as an independent nation.

INDEPENDENCE SPREADS

By 1813, wealthy criollo and revolutionary leader Simón Bolívar had seized his native Venezuela from the Spaniards. Within a few years, however, Spanish opposition forced Bolívar to flee to Jamaica. He returned with a large army to retake Venezuela in 1816. The same year, revolutionary leader José de San Martín ousted the Spaniards from his native Argentina and then crossed the Andes Mountains and liberated Chile in 1818.

Bolívar created the new republic of Gran Colombia in 1819, that consisted of Venezuela and Colombia, and served as its first president. He then joined forces with San Martín and took Panama in Central America in 1821 and Ecuador in 1822, adding those lands to Gran Colombia. The war for South America reached its climax in Peru, a Spanish stronghold. Bolívar and San Martín's armies defeated the Spaniards. Upper Peru became the new republic of Bolívar, named in Bolívar's honor. By 1826, all that remained of Spain's mighty empire in the Americas were the islands of Cuba and Puerto Rico.

SIMÓN BOLÍVAR—
LIBERATOR OF SOUTH AMERICA

Simón Bolívar has been called the George Washington of South America and for good reason. Like Washington, Bolívar was both a great military strategist and a thoughtful political leader. He envisioned a union of South American states, similar to the United States. But his Gran Colombia did not last long. One by one, the quarreling leaders in each country broke away from the union. By 1828, Bolívar was president of only what is present-day Colombia. A complex man with a strong will, Bolívar, once hailed as *El Libertador*, fell out of favor with many Latin Americans. He narrowly escaped death in an assassination attempt in Bogota, capital of Colombia, in September 1828. He retired as president of Colombia in 1830 and made plans to go into exile in France. Before he could do so, however, he died of tuberculosis—a bitter and broken man.

TROUBLE IN MEXICO

Back in Mexico, the liberators could not agree on the future of their new nation. The coalition of liberals and conservatives split apart. The conservatives, composed of mostly peninsulares and some well-to-do criollos, wanted Mexico to become a *monarchy*, ruled by a member of the

The Imperial flag of Mexico during the reign of Agustín de Iturbide.

Spanish royal family. The liberals, made up of the majority of the criollos and the mestizos, wanted Mexico to become a *republic*, ruled by a democratically elected legislature and president. General Iturbide formed his own third group, which included the military, and seized power in 1822. His true ambitions became clear, and he crowned himself Emperor Agustín I on July 21 of that year. However, Iturbide's tenure of power was brief. He was removed from office within a year by troops under the leadership of General Antonio López de Santa Anna. When Iturbide attempted to seize power a second time in 1824, he was captured and executed.

THE RISE OF SANTA ANNA

The liberals were now in control. On October 4, 1824, Mexican lawmakers drew up a *constitution*, and Mexico was proclaimed a republic. But, unlike the United States, it was a fragile republic. Centuries of autocratic Spanish rule had provided no model for a democratic government, and for the next decade the struggle between the monarchists and the republicans continued. The first elected president, Manuel Félix Fernández, also known as Guadalupe Victoria, completed his four-year term in office, but the next elected president, Manuel Gomez Pedraza, was quickly removed from office by his political rival Vicente Guerrero.

On August 13, 1829, the Spaniards made a desperate attempt to retake Mexico. A Spanish force from Cuba landed at Tampico, Mexico, and captured it. However, a Mexican army led by Santa Anna attacked and drove out the Spanish troops, making Santa Anna a national hero. Then, in December, Santa Anna led a rebellion that removed Guerrero from power. After two short-lived presidencies in their new government, the Mexicans elected Santa Anna president in 1833. Within a year he had dissolved the congress and made himself dictator of Mexico.

UNITED STATES–LATIN RELATIONS

The United States recognized Mexico, Peru, Chile, and Colombia as sovereign nations in 1822. The king of Spain joined with other European monarchs to form what they called the Holy Alliance. Their goal was to quell any similar uprisings in their own countries. The United States

feared this Holy Alliance might attempt to retake Spain's former colonies in the Americas. On December 2, 1823, U.S. president James Monroe delivered a message to Congress in which he warned that the United States would defend any independent country in the Western Hemisphere threatened by a European country. This plan became known as the Monroe Doctrine, although it had actually been drawn up by Monroe's Secretary of State, John Quincy Adams.

Mexican general Antonio López de Santa Anna defeated the Spanish at Tampico in 1829.

The Monroe
Doctrine was
signed by
(l. to r.) John
Quincy Adams,
William Harris
Crawford,
William Wirt,
President James
Monroe, John
C. Calhoun,
Daniel D.
Tompkins, and
John McLean.

The Monroe Doctrine gave hope to Simón Bolívar that the United States would become a firm friend to the new nations of Latin America. In 1826, Bolívar organized the Panama Conference, the first meeting ever of the nations of Latin America to work toward unification. He invited the United States to come and observe the conference. Members of Congress, particularly those from southern states, were opposed to U.S. representation at the conference. Colombia had abolished slavery in 1821, and many other Latin countries were planning to do the same. The economy of the American South depended on slavery, and the southern congressmen felt threatened by the stand of the Latin countries against slavery. They also feared that Bolívar might free Cuba, a Spanish colony built on slave labor where American businesses had strong economic interests. In the end, John Sargeant, an American delegate to the Panama Conference, arrived too late to participate. A second delegate, Richard C. Anderson, died en route to Panama. The bond of friendship between the United States and Mexico was a tentative one. In the 1830s, the focus of this relationship would shift to the Spanish provinces to the north, to what is now part of Mexico and the United States. These sparsely populated frontier regions had been known for centuries as the Spanish borderlands.

ACTA DE INDEPENDENCIA

DEL

IMPERIO MEXICANO

PRONUNCIADA POR SU JUNTA SOBERANA,

CONGREGADA EN LA CAPITAL DE ÉL EN 28 DE SETIEMBRE DE 1821

La Nación Mexicana, que por trescientos años, ni ha tenido voluntad propia ni libre el uso de la voz, sale hoy de la opresión en que ha vivido. Los heroicos esfuerzos de sus hijos han sido coronados, y está consumada la empresa, eternamente memorable, que un genio, superior a toda admiración y el amor y gloria de su patria, principió en Iguala, prosiguió y llevó al cabo, arrostrando obstáculos casi insuperables.

Restituida, pues, esta parte del Septentrión al ejercicio de cuantos derechos le concedió el Autor de la naturaleza y reconocen por inenajenables y sagrados las naciones cultas de la tierra, en libertad de constituirse del modo que más convenga a su felicidad, y con representantes que puedan manifestar su voluntad y sus designios, comienza a hacer uso de tan preciosos dones, y declara solemnemente, por medio de la Junta Suprema del Imperio, que es Nación soberana é independiente de la antigua España, con quien, en lo sucesivo, no mantendrá otra unión que la de una amistad estrecha, en los términos que prescribieren los tratados; que entablará relaciones amistosas con las demás potencias, ejecutando, respecto de ellas, cuantos actos pueden y están en posesión de ejecutar las otras naciones soberanas; que va a constituirse con arreglo a las bases que en el plan de Iguala y tratado de Córdoba estableció sabiamente el primer jefe del ejército imperial de las tres garantías; y en fin, que sostendrá a todo trance, y con el sacrificio de los haberes y vidas de sus individuos, si fuere necesario, esta solemne declaración; hecha en la Capital del imperio a veintiocho de setiembre del año de mil ochocientos veintiuno, primero de la independencia mexicana.

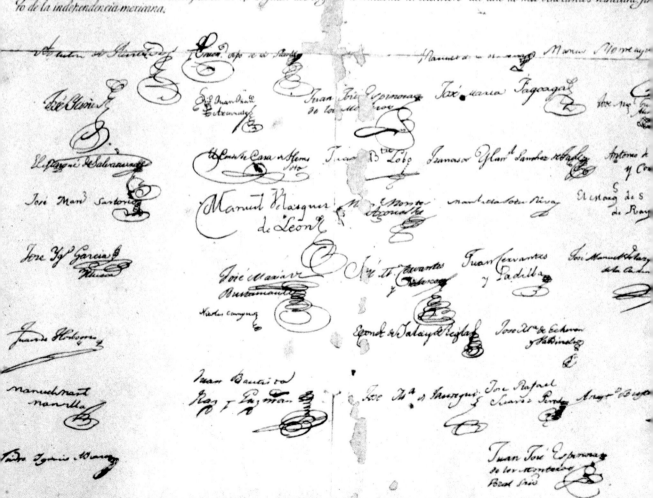

CHAPTER FOUR

RESTLESSNESS IN THE BORDERLANDS

WHEN MEXICO WON ITS INDEPENDENCE from Spain in 1821, it inherited an empire. The northern Spanish provinces of California, New Mexico, and Texas—collectively known as the borderlands— were now in its possession. For most of the people who lived in the borderlands, independence was greeted with muted enthusiasm, indifference, or even regret. Mexico City, its society, and culture, was hundreds of miles away and seemingly as remote as the moon. The people of the borderlands had little representation in the colonial congress. The Spanish had largely left them alone to live as they chose, but when they needed protection, the Spanish troops had been there to defend them from their greatest peril—the Native Americans.

Opposite: A copy of the Declaration of Independence when Mexico became free from Spain.

The borderlands were just that, a rugged frontier on the border of the Spanish empire. As late as the early 1800s, there were fewer than 20,000 people of Spanish descent living in this vast region.

There was a brief rebellion in Texas in 1813 against the Spanish, but it was led not by Mexican rebels but by a former U.S. Army officer, Augustus Magee, and a wealthy criollo, Bernardo Gutiérrez, living in New Orleans. The rebellion failed. There was no such serious attempt to revolt against Spain in New Mexico. In California, when a *privateer* entered Monterey Bay in 1818 and called for *Californios* to support the overthrow of Spain, they flatly refused, and the rebels burned down their town.

LAND OF MISSIONS

For the two centuries after Spanish explorer Juan Cabrillo landed in California in 1542 and claimed it for Spain, it had largely remained unexplored. It took the threat of another colonial power to rouse the Spanish to begin settlements. For decades, Russian fur traders had been working their way down the Pacific coast from what is present-day Alaska, and by the 1740s, they had entered northern California. Fearing the Russians would seize California from them, Spain sent out one exploratory party after another to find good sites for settlements.

In 1769, Captain Gaspar de Portolá, governor of Baja (Lower) California, the only part of the province with per-

The California mission San Diego de Alcalá is the home of the first church in California.

manent settlements, led an exploratory party north. Portolá built a *presidio*, or military fort, at the present-day site of San Diego. In Portolá's party was an energetic Franciscan priest, Father Junípero Serra. Serra and other Spanish priests saw it as their mission to convert the Native Americans to Christianity. Under order of the Spanish Crown, Serra built the first California *mission* in what is present-day San Diego. The mission was a religious community where converted Native Americans could be taught a craft or trade and then work for the mission in return for food and shelter.

Over the next fifty-four years, Padre Serra and his followers built a chain of twenty-one Spanish missions, stretching from San Diego north to present-day Sonoma, all within about a day's walk from each other. The missions brought order and prosperity to California. By 1802, there were nearly 25,000 Christians, both Spanish and Native American, in California, most of them living in the missions. Some of the missions grew to be important cities. Yerba Buena, founded in 1776, later became the city of San Francisco, and Los Angeles was founded in 1781. The last Spanish mission in California was built at Sonoma in 1823.

The missions were a mixed blessing for the estimated 30,000 Native Americans who lived and worked in them by the 1820s. They may have learned a meaningful trade or craft, and gained a new religion, Christianity, but they were then often forced to work long hours for the mission. Of the thousands of Native-American deaths recorded at the missions, many were from being overworked and from contracting diseases that came from Europe, which were spread by unsanitary conditions. This led some Spanish settlers to criticize the mission system as inhumane.

Spanish expansion in California did not end the Russian threat, however. In 1812, the Russians established Fort Ross on the northern California coast. But what the Spanish could not stop, the Americans did. The Monroe Doctrine of 1823 stated that any European intrusion in the Americas would be seen as a hostile act and dealt with aggressively by the United States. American forces convinced the Russians to get out of California. The following year, the Russians agreed to stay in their colony of Alaska,

although some of them remained in the Pacific coastal region for nearly another fifteen years.

The Russian Fort Ross, on the northern coast of California.

DAY OF THE VAQUERO

One way the missions supported themselves was by the raising of cattle. The missions sold the cattle for their meat, their hides, used for clothing and shoes, and their fat, called tallow, for the raw material of candles, soap, and other products. They hired Mexican horsemen called *vaqueros* to tend the cattle, brand them to identify ownership, and drive them on the trail to market. Vaquero is from the Spanish word *vaca*, meaning cow. The vaqueros were the first cowboys, and later, American cowboys adopted the clothing and equipment the vaqueros had developed for their rough work.

Vaqueros wore leather overalls called *chaparajos*, or chaps, that protected their legs from the rough and thorny brush and plants they rode through on the trail. A bandana was a kind of neckerchief that could be tied around the head in winter to keep a vaquero's head warm. It could also be wrapped around the mouth and nose to keep out dust kicked up by the cattle. The sombrero was a large hat with a wide brim. It protected the vaquero's head from the blazing heat of the sun or from wind and rain.

A typical vaquero from the mid-1800s.

The vaquero used *una reata*, a rope, to lasso a cow for branding. In English, the word became lariat. Both cattle and horses were kept in a *corral*, Spanish for circle. Sometimes the vaqueros held contests among themselves to see who was the best at roping cattle or riding a wild horse, known as a bronco. They called these contests rodeos and they eventually became the popular sporting events still enjoyed in the western United States and Canada today.

THE RISE OF RANCHOS

As more and more Spanish settlers moved north into Alta (Upper) California (the present-day state of California), they wanted land on which to raise crops and cattle. Much of the developed land was in the hands of the Roman Catholic Church, that owned the missions. Criticism against the mission system grew. Many people, including the Spanish Crown, saw it as an obstacle to progress in the province. In 1834, the Mexican government seized control of the missions, and transformed them into churches, houses of worship that were no longer self-sufficient communities. Mexico also turned some of the mission property into large estates and gave or sold them to wealthy landowners. These well-to-do Californios became *rancheros* and set up large *ranchos* to raise cattle. They employed the vaqueros who had previously worked for the missions. By 1834, there were more than 30,000 vaqueros tending some 396,000 head of cattle in California, Texas, and Mexico. Native Americans, who once worked and lived in the missions, were hired as workers and servants by the rancheros. They were often treated harshly and would occasionally rebel, attacking ranchos and settlements.

In 1822, when Mexico took control of California, the rancheros looked to the Mexican government for help from raiding Native Americans, but received little or none. Governors sent from Mexico were often strict and dictatorial to all the Californios. A grassroots effort against the hated Governor Manuel Victoria in 1831 forced him to resign and leave California. Mexican control over its most economically rich province was growing weaker and weaker.

PEDRO FAGES,
GOVERNOR OF CALIFORNIA

Among the more popular and colorful Spanish governors of Alta California was Pedro Fages. A native of Catalonia, Spain, Fages served twice as governor, from 1770 to 1774 and again from 1782 to 1791. Unlike some of the Spanish governors of New Spain, Fages was no office-bound administrator. He was a seasoned frontiersman and an experienced hunter whose skill at hunting bears earned him the nickname *El Orso*, which means The Bear. Though hot-tempered with subordinates at times, Fages was always kind and warm to children and loved to give them candy. He also had progressive ideas. In 1790, he proposed that his superior contact U.S. president George Washington about the building of a road across North America from California to Virginia. The road was never built, and Fages retired to Mexico in 1791. He died there three years later.

American traders then were moving west to California, many of them becoming Mexican citizens and marrying into Californios families. The growing wealth of this region did not escape the attention of the United States. In 1835, U.S. president Andrew Jackson, who fifteen years earlier was instrumental in bringing Florida into the United States, offered to buy part of California. The Mexican government turned him down.

REMOTE TEXAS

Texas, the largest of the Spanish borderlands, was also the most sparsely settled. By the end of the 1700s, after more than one hundred years of colonization, there were only about seven thousand Spanish settlers, or *Tejanos*, in all of Texas. There were good reasons for this, however. This land was the farthest province from central Mexico. It was a rugged, rocky, desertlike region, much of it not fit for farming. It was also dangerous. The Spanish may have owned Texas, but the southern plains of northwest Texas were the hunting grounds of the Comanche Indians. These fierce warriors periodically attacked the often defenseless settlements and ranchos, burning, pillaging, and killing. Who would want to leave the comforts of Mexico to go live in this distant, dangerous land?

In one way, the Spanish did not mind that Texas was empty. As a wasteland, it could serve as a barrier to intruders, such as Americans, who might want to seize Mexico with its

THE COMANCHE

The word Comanche comes from a Ute word *kohmaht*, meaning people. The Comanche were the dominant people of the southwest plains of the United States. Because they followed the buffalo, which they hunted on horseback, the Comanche were expert riders and fearless fighters. A Comanche warrior in battle would dodge arrows and bullets by hanging on the side of his pony or even slipping under its belly.

Although Texas contained the most Comanche, they also roamed across Oklahoma, New Mexico, Colorado, and Kansas. Unlike some Native American tribes, the Comanche never united into a single nation, but were split into a dozen separate groups. With no strong single leader, they fought among themselves as much as with the Spaniards, Mexicans, and Anglo settlers.

In 1867, the Comanche signed the Medicine Lodge Treaty with the United States government and agreed to move to a reservation in Oklahoma, where most of the almost ten thousand remaining Comanche live today as farmers, ranchers, teachers, and other professionals.

rich gold and silver mines. But as time went on, the lack of settlements made Texas such a no-man's land that the Spanish had to do something to hold on to it—they would need pioneers to populate it. But where would these new settlers come from? A generation of young Mexican males had been largely wiped out in the ongoing war of independence. And European immigrants preferred to settle in more populated areas where they could live with others of their nationality. So, the Spanish government turned to the more adventurous people of the United States to help settle this land that no one else seemed to want.

Stephen Fuller Austin created an Anglo community in Texas in the early 1820s.

STEPHEN AUSTIN AND THE AMERICAN COLONIES

Among the first Americans to take up the Spanish offer to move to Texas was former miner and Missouri banker Moses Austin. In 1820, Austin entered into a contract with the Spanish to establish his own Anglo colony on a tract of land along the Brazos River in southeastern Texas. But then, two unforeseen events happened: Spain lost Mexico and Texas to the Mexican rebels, and Moses Austin died.

Austin's son, Stephen, however, was as enterprising as his father had been, and he convinced the new Mexican government to honor the land grant that the Spanish made with his father. Under Austin's leadership, three hundred Anglo families moved to a large tract of land along the Brazos River in 1821. In 1823, Austin established San Felipe de Austin, the seat of government of his little colony. As Austin's colony expanded with more land grants, other *empresarios*, as the Mexicans called them, led their own groups to southeastern Texas. Soon there were dozens of growing, thriving Anglo communities. Many of these newcomers preferred

Stephen F. Austin (standing in dark coat) issues land grants to colonists of Texas.

the easy going government of the Mexicans to that of the United States. The Anglo settlers were allowed to use slave labor to raise crops, as were the owners of large farms in the American South. However, these settlers had to agree to convert to Catholicism and become loyal Mexican citizens. They paid little or no tax to the Mexican government and were generally left alone.

By 1830, the population of Texas had swelled to about 21,000 people, only a few thousand of whom were Tejanos. The rest were American settlers and about four thousand black slaves that they owned. This alarmed the Mexican government, however. If the flow of American immigrants continued, soon the Americans might seize Texas. So, in 1830, the Mexicans prohibited further immigration into Texas. But by then it was too late to stop the flow of immigrants. More and more Americans were heading west, many of them traveling beyond Texas, along a trail that would take them to the capital of the third and oldest of the Spanish borderlands—New Mexico.

CHAPTER FIVE

New Mexico and the Santa Fe Trail

NEW MEXICO, WHICH AT THAT TIME ALSO included present-day Arizona, was the oldest of the Spanish borderlands. Santa Fe, its capital, was founded by Spanish explorers in 1610 on the site of an old Pueblo village in north central New Mexico. For a century, Santa Fe remained a remote outpost in the Spanish empire. In the 1700s, settlers from Mexico slowly began to make the trek north to the colony, founding such settlements as Taos, Santa Cruz, and Albuquerque. Like Texas, life in New Mexico was rugged and difficult. Apache and Navajo tribes resented the newcomers who came to live on their tribal lands and attacked settlements and farms.

Opposite:
Apache Indians raided Spanish settlements for food and land.

THE NUEVOMEXICANOS

The Spanish people who lived in New Mexico, the *nuevomexicanos*, were a hardy and independent breed. Unlike California, New Mexico had few large ranchos or farms. Most settlers were mestizos, who worked small farms or herded sheep. There was a small upper class made up of *patrones*, recruiters for settlements who then took over the responsibility of governing the small communities and defending them from attacks by the Native Americans. But New Mexican society was surprisingly flexible. A mestizo who worked hard could rise in social class to become a large landholder. One of the most successful was Manuel Armijo who started out in New Mexico as a poor vaquero and over time became a wealthy sheepherder. He eventually became governor of the province.

Governor Manuel Armijo, a distinguished mestizo.

The nuevomexicanos were living in a frontier society where there were few manufactured products to buy. They relied on trading with others to get the goods they needed. Large villages had craftspeople who made religious objects called *santos*, woven rugs and clothing, and other crafts. People would come to a town square regularly to trade with one another for goods. In autumn, the largest trading fair took place at Taos, just north of Santa Fe. Villagers from all over New Mexico would come to buy and sell goods. The Taos Fair also attracted Native Americans, Mexican merchants, who brought manufactured goods to sell, and Anglo and French trappers, who traded furs for food they would need to get through the long winter months.

UNWELCOME VISITORS

By the early 1800s, peace and stability were finally coming to New Mexico. The Spanish officials made peace treaties with the Ute and Comanche tribes. With fewer attacks, more Anglo trappers and traders were willing to make the long journey to Santa Fe to trade their goods with the eager New Mexicans. But Spanish officials were distrustful of these visitors from the United States. They accused them of spying for the U.S. government, which the Spanish believed was plotting to seize their territory.

In 1806, U.S. Army Lieutenant Zebulon M. Pike led a small party of soldiers into Mexican territory from Louisiana and built a fort. The Spanish captured Pike and his men and took them to Santa Fe. Under interrogation, Pike denied that he was spying and claimed to be only seeking a shorter route for traders to the southwest. The Spaniards did not believe him and kept him a prisoner for several months.

NEW MEXICO'S FOLK ARTISTS—
THE SANTEROS

Among the most skilled craftspeople of colonial New Mexico were the *santeros*, folk artists who created santos—religious paintings or carved statues. Santos were originally brought to Mexico from Spain and used by the Spanish missionaries to teach indios about Christianity and the lives of Jesus and the saints. Later, the missionaries made their own Santos and taught the art to the villagers.

The first native-born nuevomexicano to become a santeros was Pedro Antonio Fresquis, who was born in 1749 and lived and worked in Truchas, near Santa Fe. Fresquis's highly stylized religious paintings are called *retablos*, and those that survive today can be seen in museums. Little is known of Fresquis's life or that of any other early Santeros. Many of them remain nameless, known only by where they lived and worked, such as "the Laguna santero." A santero's paintings and statues were displayed in village churches, homes, and open spaces for worship called *morades*.

By the early 1900s, the making of santos was a dying art. More recently, the art has been revived by a new generation of santeros in New Mexico, who have brought their own modern sensibilities and styles to this age-old art of the Spanish southwest.

During this time, they took Pike on a tour of Mexican cities and towns to impress him with their strength. When he was released, Pike brought back stories of Mexican wealth and the vastness of the land, especially of Texas, that encouraged more Americans to head for the southwest.

As the number of traders in Santa Fe grew, the Spanish treated them more harshly than they had treated Pike. One group in 1812 was arrested and spent nine years in prison. Such treatment of American citizens increased tensions between the United States and Spain.

Zebulon Montgomery Pike was an explorer who searched for the source of the Mississippi River.

WILLIAM BECKNELL FINDS A WAY

William Becknell was an enterprising frontiersman who traded with the Native Americans. Unlike some of the other men who did so, Becknell was fair and honest and gained the Native Americans' respect and trust. In the fall of 1821, Becknell was on his way to trade with Native Americans in the west, when his four-man pack train came upon two Mexicans near the Arkansas River. When the Mexicans saw Becknell's supply of goods, they told him he could gain more profit trading with the Mexicans at Santa Fe than with

ARIZONA—
THE FORGOTTEN BORDERLAND

The western part of New Mexico, present-day Arizona, had few settlements. Jesuit priest and missionary Eusebio Kino came to this desolate region with its rocky canyons and mountains in 1687 and over the next decade and a half established several missions. These missions enjoyed little of the peace and prosperity that the California missions had. The Apache and Navajo were a constant threat. The mission of San José de Tumacacori was burned to the ground by Apaches in 1769. The first true Spanish settlement was not established in Arizona until 1752 at Tubac. The second, Tucson, built in 1776, was begun as a fort. Its thick adobe walls offered the soldiers and their families protection from the Native Americans, making Tucson the only walled city in what is now the United States. As late as the 1820s, these remained the only Spanish settlements in this desolate half of New Mexico.

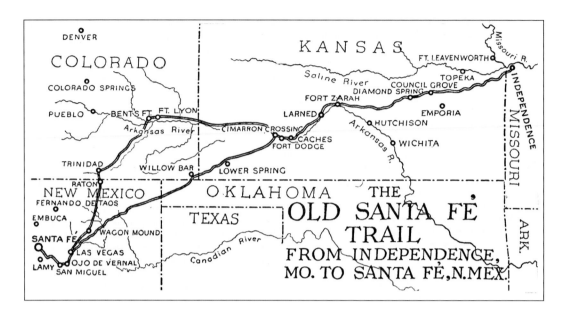

A map showing the Santa Fe Trail.

the Native Americans. They told him that since the Mexicans had gained their independence from Spain, they were now more welcoming to Anglo traders than the Spanish had been.

Becknell took their advice and forged a new trail across the West to Santa Fe. The trail Becknell blazed was largely one explored by Spaniard Pedro Vial in 1792, but Becknell turned it into a byway. His Santa Fe Trail began in Independence, Missouri, and followed the western branch of the Missouri River into Kansas. At Cimarron Crossing, the trail split. The northern route continued into Colorado and then south to New Mexico. The southern route followed the Cimarron River across the end of the Oklahoma panhandle and then southwest to Santa Fe.

On his arrival in Santa Fe, Becknell was greeted enthusiastically by the New Mexicans. In a short time, he had

traded all the goods he was carrying and then stayed the winter in the easygoing capital. On his return, Becknell quickly organized a second expedition, this time with wagons, so he could carry more goods. On his third trip, in 1824, he took on two partners, both successful merchants. This expedition included twenty-five wagons, 150 horses and mules, and $30,000 worth of merchandise.

Families and traders journeyed along the Santa Fe Trail in covered wagons.

The Santa Fe Trail was soon crowded with traders who hoped to make as much money with their goods as Becknell had with his. As traders increased in number, the Mexican government became concerned.

RENEWED TENSIONS

Manuel Armijo was appointed governor of New Mexico in 1827. Armijo expressed his dislike for Anglo traders by putting a tax of five hundred dollars per wagon on goods brought to Santa Fe. Small traders could not afford the tax and left the Santa Fe market to the larger traders. Armijo then passed a law forbidding foreigners from hunting or trapping in Mexican territory. He also began to arrest traders and confiscate their goods.

In 1832, the year that William Becknell died, there were about 25,000 Anglo Americans living in Texas alone and thousands more in New Mexico and California. A good many of these Americans arrived there by traveling the Santa Fe Trail. Fearing more would come, Mexico closed its border to foreigners that year.

As the period of the New Republic drew to a close, the tensions between Mexico and the United States remained unresolved. The Anglos in Texas would soon rise up and rebel against the Mexican government to create their own independent republic. The tensions in the other border-lands of California and New Mexico would continue to build until war erupted between the United States and Mexico. The Mexican-American War (1846–1848) would change the face of the Spanish southwest forever.

Timeline

1769	Father Junípero Serra builds the first of California's twenty-one missions in San Diego.
1775	The American Revolution begins.
1776	Tucson is founded by the Spanish in present-day Arizona.
1779	Spain declares war on Great Britain and recognizes the American colonies; Louisiana governor Bernardo de Gálvez captures three British forts along the Mississippi River.
1780	Gálvez captures British forts at Mobile and Pensacola along the Gulf of Mexico.
1781	Los Angeles is founded in Alta (Upper) California.
1783	Spain regains Florida from the British in the Peace Treaty of Paris.
1795	Spain agrees to the 31st parallel as Florida's northern border with the United States.
1800	France takes Louisiana back from Spain and sells it to the Americans three years later.
1806	United States Army lieutenant Zebulon Pike is captured by Spanish troops and accused of spying in the Spanish borderlands.
1810	The Mexican War of Independence begins under the leadership of Father Miguel Hidalgo.
1818	U.S. General Andrew Jackson invades Spanish Florida, captures two Spanish forts, and usurps the Spanish governor.
1819	Spain and the United States sign the Adams-Onís Treaty, under which Spain gives Florida to the United States.
1821	Mexico declares its independence from Spain on February 24; Anglo settlers establish two American settlements in Texas under the leadership of Stephen Austin; William Becknell makes his first trading expedition along the Santa Fe Trail.
1823	The Monroe Doctrine warns European powers to stay out of the Americas.
1824	Mexico declares itself a republic.
1830	The Mexican government forbids further immigration to Texas and New Mexico from the United States.
1834	The Mexican government seizes the California missions and turns them into churches and estates; General Antonio Lopez de Santa Anna is elected president of Mexico.

GLOSSARY

annex To incorporate territory into the domain of a country.

Californios Spanish settlers in California.

constitution A document stating the laws by which a nation is governed.

Creoles Members of the French-speaking urban population of Louisiana descended from the earliest French, Spanish, and African-American settlers.

criollos Persons born in Spanish America of Spanish ancestry.

empresarios Anglo Americans responsible for colonies in Spanish Texas.

indios Native Americans living under Spanish rule in Spanish America.

mestizos Persons of mixed Native American and Spanish ancestry.

mission A self-contained religious community where Native Americans were converted, educated, and put to work under the direction of priests.

monarchy A state or nation ruled by a king or queen.

mulattoes Persons of mixed African and Caucasian ancestry.

nuevomexicanos Early Spanish settlers of New Mexico.

parishes Counties in Louisiana.

patrones Community leaders in the Spanish borderlands.

peninsulares Persons in Spanish America born in Spain; members of the ruling class.

presidio A military fort in Spanish America.

privateer A privately owned ship authorized to fight enemy ships.

rancheros Wealthy owners of ranchos.

ranchos Large cattle ranches in Spanish America.

republic A state run by a government representative of its people.

santos Religious folk paintings or statues made in the Spanish southwest.

santeros Folk artists who make santos.

sovereignty Independent power in or of a state.

Tejanos Spanish settlers in Texas.

Tories Americans who supported the British in the American Revolution and often went into exile afterward.

vaquero A Spanish-American cowboy.

viceroy An appointed ruler in Spanish America who represented the Spanish king.

FURTHER INFORMATION

BOOKS

Kachur, Matthew and Jon Sterngass. *Spanish Settlement in North America 1824–1898* (Latino-American History). New York: Chelsea House, 2007.

Roberts, Russell. *Bernardo de Galvez* (Latinos in American History). Hockessin, DE: Mitchell Lane Publishers, 2004.

Whiting, Jim. *Junipero Jose Serra* (Latinos in American History). Hockessin, DE: Mitchell Lane Publishers, 2004.

Worth, Richard. *Independence for Latino America 1776–1823*. New York: Chelsea House, 2006.

WEB SITES

Coloquio

www.coloquio.com

An exhaustive timeline of Hispanic involvement in American history from the 14th century to the present, complied by Dr. Juan M. Pérez of the Hispanic Division of the Library of Congress.

Hispanic Online

www.hispaniconline.com

A useful site with information and brief articles about Latino history, culture, food, and other areas of interest.

BIBLIOGRAPHY

Heidler, David Stephen and Jeanne T. Heidler. *Old Hickory's War: Andrew Jackson and the Quest for Empire*. Baton Rouge: Louisiana State University Press, 2003.

Novas, Himilce. *Everything You Need to Know About Latino History: 2008 Edition*. New York: Plume, 2007.

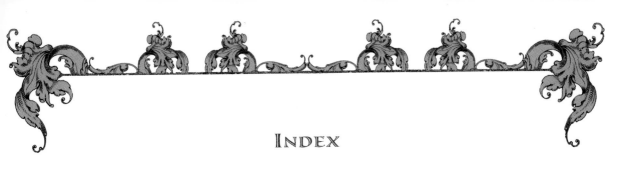

Index

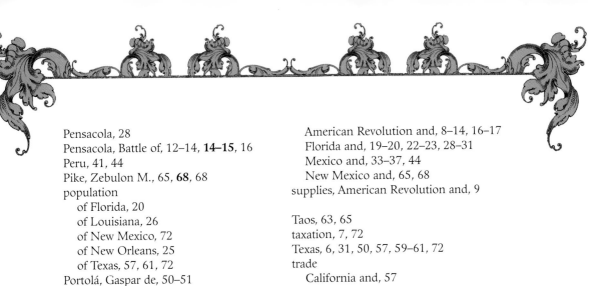

About the Author

STEVEN OTFINOSKI has written *Hispanics in U.S. History Vol. 2—1865 to Present* for Globe Book Company and, more recently, *Latinos in the Arts* for Facts On File. He is also the author of *Francisco Coronado: In Search of the Seven Cities of Gold*, *Vasco Nunez de Balboa: Explorer of the Pacific*, and *Juan Ponce de Leon: Discoverer of Florida* in Marshall Cavendish's Great Explorations series.